9/13

‖‖‖ ‖‖‖‖‖‖‖‖‖‖‖‖‖‖‖‖‖‖ ‖‖‖

W9-ANT-086

WINTER

Stephanie Turnbull

Published by Smart Apple Media
P.O. Box 1329
Mankato, MN 56002

Printed in the United States of America, at
Corporate Graphics in North Mankato, Minnesota.

Designed by Hel James
Edited by Mary-Jane Wilkins

Library of Congress Cataloging-in-Publication Data

Turnbull, Stephanie.
  Winter / by Stephanie Turnbull.
    p. cm. -- (The seasons)
  Includes bibliographical references and index.
  Summary: "Uses photos to help describe the changes
that happen to the weather, plants, and animals in
winter. Mentions the holidays and events that usually
occur in winter months"--Provided by publisher.
  Audience: Grades K-3.
  ISBN 978-1-59920-850-3 (hbk., library bound : alk.
paper)
  1. Winter--Juvenile literature. I. Title.
  QB637.8.T87 2013
  508.2--dc23
                            2012004121

Photo acknowledgements
t = top, b = bottom
page 1 karen roach/Shutterstock; 3 iStockphoto/
Thinkstock; 5 Alinute Silzeviciute/Shutterstock;
6 Pukhov Konstantin/Shutterstock; 7 Govorov Pavel/
Shutterstock; 8 iStockphoto/Thinkstock; 9 Zurijeta/
Shutterstock; 11 iStockphoto/Thinkstock;
12 iStockphoto/Thinkstock; 13 Douglas Freer/
Shutterstock; 14 iStockphoto/Thinkstock;
15 Al Mueller/Shutterstock; 16t Tony Campbell/
Shutterstock, b Jupiterimages/Thinkstock;
17 visceralimage/Shutterstock; 18 Zolran/
Shutterstock; 19 Couperfield/Shutterstock;
20 Jupiterimages/Thinkstock; 21 pio3/Shutterstock;
22 Anest/Shutterstock; 21 Digital Vision/Thinkstock,
hearts Dalibor Sevaljevic/Shutterstock
Cover Hemera/Thinkstock

DAD0505
042012
9 8 7 6 5 4 3 2 1

Contents

It's Winter!

A hungry
deer sniffs the
frozen air.

Brrrr!

Our winter months are December, January, and February.

The sun rises late every morning and sets early every evening. Days feel short and chilly.

Wear layers of warm clothes in winter. Don't forget a hat!

Ice Everywhere

On very cold winter days, water freezes into ice. Long icicles hang from buildings.

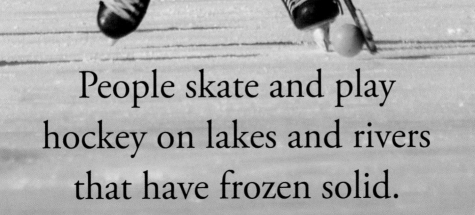

People skate and play hockey on lakes and rivers that have frozen solid.

White World

Sometimes water droplets in the air freeze together to make snowflakes. Softly they f
       l
        u
         t
          t
           e
            r

to the ground.

New snow sparkles in the sun. It crunches and squeaks as you plod through it.

Wild Weather

Winter can be stormy. Strong winds and heavy snow make swirling blizzards.

Sometimes rain or hailstones hammer down.

Lots of snow may block roads. Snow plows work hard to clear them.

Take a Break

Many trees and plants
stop growing in winter.

They look dead, but under the ground their roots are alive. A blanket of snow protects them.

A few plants have winter berries or even flowers.

Hungry Animals

Winter is a
tough time for
animals. There
is less food to
eat and water
may be frozen.

Help birds survive
the winter by
giving them
nuts, seeds,
and water.

Keeping Warm

Birds fluff up their feathers to stay warm.

Some animals grow thicker fur. This Arctic fox has brown fur in summer...

…and thick, white
fur in winter. Now
it can hide in snow!

Cozy Homes

Many animals make snug winter dens under the snow and curl up inside.

Some creatures go into a deep sleep.

These bats are sleeping in a cave.

A ferret pops up
from its den to
look for food.

Winter Fun

There is lots to do in winter. Many people celebrate Christmas, then the start of a new year.

Enjoy winter by sledding, spotting animals, or snuggling up indoors with a book!

Did You Know...?

When we have winter,
it is summer in the
southern half of
the world.

Every snowflake has
six points made of
tiny ice crystals.

Wood frogs freeze
solid in winter
and melt in spring.

February 14 is Valentine's
Day, when you can send
cards to people you love!

Useful Words

blizzard
A big snowstorm
with strong winds.

hailstone
A tiny ball of frozen rain.

winter
The time of year, called
a season, after fall and
before spring.

den
A hole or nest where
animals shelter and hide.

Index